small towns. They enjoy a slower way of life.

Many people in small towns have their own businesses. They may own a general store. Others have butcher shops and bakeries. Some people run their own restaurants or cafés. Family members often work together. Some businesses are passed down through **generations**.

People who build or fix things can start a business in a small town. Carpenters, electricians, and plumbers work in houses and other buildings. Mechanics are needed to repair cars. Other businesses include day cares, hair salons, and flower shops.

Like big cities, small towns have many service jobs. Doctors and nurses help keep people well. Dentists make sure people's teeth are healthy. Police officers help keep everyone safe. Principals and teachers work with students.

Small towns do not have many people. This makes it easy to get to know the people who work in them. Many workers are neighbours and friends.

Some small towns look for new people to move to them. They may seek people who have skills that others in town do not have. These people may be welders or sewers. They may be woodworkers. Some of the people who come to small towns are **immigrants**. They may start their own businesses in a small town.

Most small towns cannot afford to pay firefighters. Instead, the fire department is made up of part-time **volunteers**. These people also work at a different job. The volunteers must still go through a training program. The program takes many hours to complete.

Chapter Two

THE GREAT OUTDOORS

Canada has a lot of natural resources. These are things that come from the land or ocean. Many small towns are built near these resources.

Soil is a natural resource. We need good soil to grow food. The best soils in Canada are on the prairies. Some people in small towns are farmers. They grow crops, such as wheat and corn. Others grow oats, barley, or **canola**.

Some resources come from deep under the ground. We get them by mining. Mines are found all across Canada. Uranium, potash, coal, and diamonds come from mines. Some workers remove these products from the earth. Others help make them usable.

Some farmers sell their crops at local markets.

The paper mill in Espanola, Ontario, was built in 1905. It has been updated with new technology over the years.

Many people use technology in their mining jobs. Some work with computers. Others control robots that work under the ground.

Some small towns are near the Atlantic Ocean. Many people in these towns are fishers. They catch fish, lobsters, crabs, shrimp, and scallops. Fishers sell some of the seafood in town. They also sell it to other places in Canada.

Boreal forests are mostly made up of trees that have needles and cones. These forests are a natural resource. They grow all over Canada, except in the Arctic and on the prairies. Loggers chop down trees. Then they collect the wood. Carpenters use some of the wood to make furniture and buildings. It is also used to make paper in paper **mills**. Some workers run the machines that make the paper. Others ship it to different places.

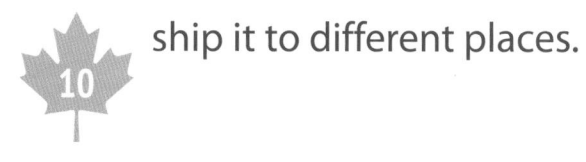

We need to use natural resources. But we must take care of the Earth, too. Tree planters replant trees in the forests. Scientists work to keep the water healthy for fish. They keep it free of waste.

Some small towns are near **national parks**. Fort Smith is near Wood Buffalo National Park in the Northwest Territories. Banff is near Banff National Park. National parks are made to protect land from being overused. Park wardens keep things running smoothly. They make sure people follow the rules. They can help in an emergency. This might be a forest fire or bear sighting.

MINING FOR CARS AND COMPUTERS

We don't have to dig for cars and computers. But some workers in small towns dig for the materials to make them. We use minerals and metals from mines to make many things. Copper is used for car motors, wires, and brakes. Silicon is used in computers. Zinc is used in sunscreen and medical creams. Nickel is used to make batteries and musical instruments. Coal and uranium are used to make electricity. Gold and diamonds are used for jewellery.

There are more than 600 Aboriginal communities in Canada. These small towns are called reserves. For many Aboriginal Peoples, the forests are their home and hunting grounds. Aboriginal forestry groups work to protect the land. They work with businesses to help them use the resources wisely.

Chapter Three

COME AND CREATE

Some people think art is only found in big cities. But those who live in small towns know better. Many artists live in small towns. They open shops, **galleries**, and studios to sell their work. Hudson is a small town in Quebec. More than half of Hudson's businesses involve arts and crafts. Legal, Alberta, is another small town. It has 35 French-themed murals on walls and buildings.

Small town artists come from all different backgrounds. They work with many types of materials. Some use paint. Others sculpt with clay. There are **glassblowers** and potters.

Nearly 140,000 people work as artists in Canada.

Aboriginal artists sell their artwork in small town galleries. Inuit artists make carvings from soapstone. Métis artists are known for their beadwork. People buy totem poles, jewellery, masks, and carvings.

Some small towns are known for their arts community. Artists and craftspeople create new things. Actors, dancers, and other performers work there. Musicians, singers, and composers live in small towns, too. Writers can find quiet places to think and work.

STAYING WARM IN STYLE

Some small town shops sell authentic Cowichan sweaters. They are made by the Cowichan First Nation on Vancouver Island. Every sweater is different. The knitters use a special method to make them. They combine traditional Aboriginal spinning and weaving with European knitting. This skill is passed down through the generations.

Bella Coola, British Columbia, is known for its Aboriginal artwork.

15

TOURING THE TOWNS

People who live in cities often visit small towns. The towns help them escape their busy schedules. Many people retire to small towns. **Tourists** are welcome in small towns. Some people work to make their visit special.

A walk through town can be fun for tourists. Store owners offer unique items in their galleries and specialty shops. Visitors can browse through antique stores. They can stop in a coffee shop or buy vegetables at a **farmers' market**.

Some people plan outdoor activities for tourists. In the summer, tourists can rent a cabin in Ontario. They can hire hiking and fishing guides. They can try surfing

Hurontario Street is the main shopping area of Collingwood, Ontario.

More than three million tourists visit Banff National Park in Alberta each year. Many of them also visit the town of Banff.

in Nova Scotia on the east coast. They can surf in British Columbia on the west coast. Visitors to British Columbia can go scuba diving, too. They can take tours in boats. They look for wildlife, such as grey whales and sea lions. In Churchill, Manitoba, tourists can see beluga whales in summer and polar bears in the fall. In the winter visitors in the northern parts of Canada can go skiing, ice skating, or sledding.

Some small towns have been around for a long time. Many of their buildings are more than 100 years old. People like to visit old

stores and churches. They go to see **historical** sites, such as grain elevators and train stations. They may go to museums. In New Brunswick, tourists visit covered bridges.

Visitors in a small town need a place to stay. Hotels hire people to work during the tourist seasons. The busiest season is from June through August. Some places are busy in the winter, too. Ski resorts, such as Whistler, British Columbia, have a lot of visitors from December through March. Hotel owners need people to work the front desk and clean the rooms. They want to make sure the tourists have a nice stay. They want them to come back again.

Canada's small towns offer all of the services people need to live. People can get to know their neighbours. They can enjoy a quieter atmosphere than in cities.

EXPLORING NUNAVUT

You can't get to the Arctic territory of Nunavut by car. You must get there by plane or boat. Most of the residents in Nunavut are Inuit. Visitors to their small towns can enjoy many outdoor activities. They can go camping, kayaking, hiking, and skiing. They can even try dogsledding.

INQUIRY QUESTIONS

What are some jobs in a small town that are connected to the environment? How are these jobs different from those in a small town in another region?

19

A SMALL TOWN IN CANADA

LAKE

SCHOOL

RESTAURANTS

COFFEE

SHOP

Burger

PARK

1 CM = 0.5 KM

— = ROUTE TO SCHOOL

N W E S

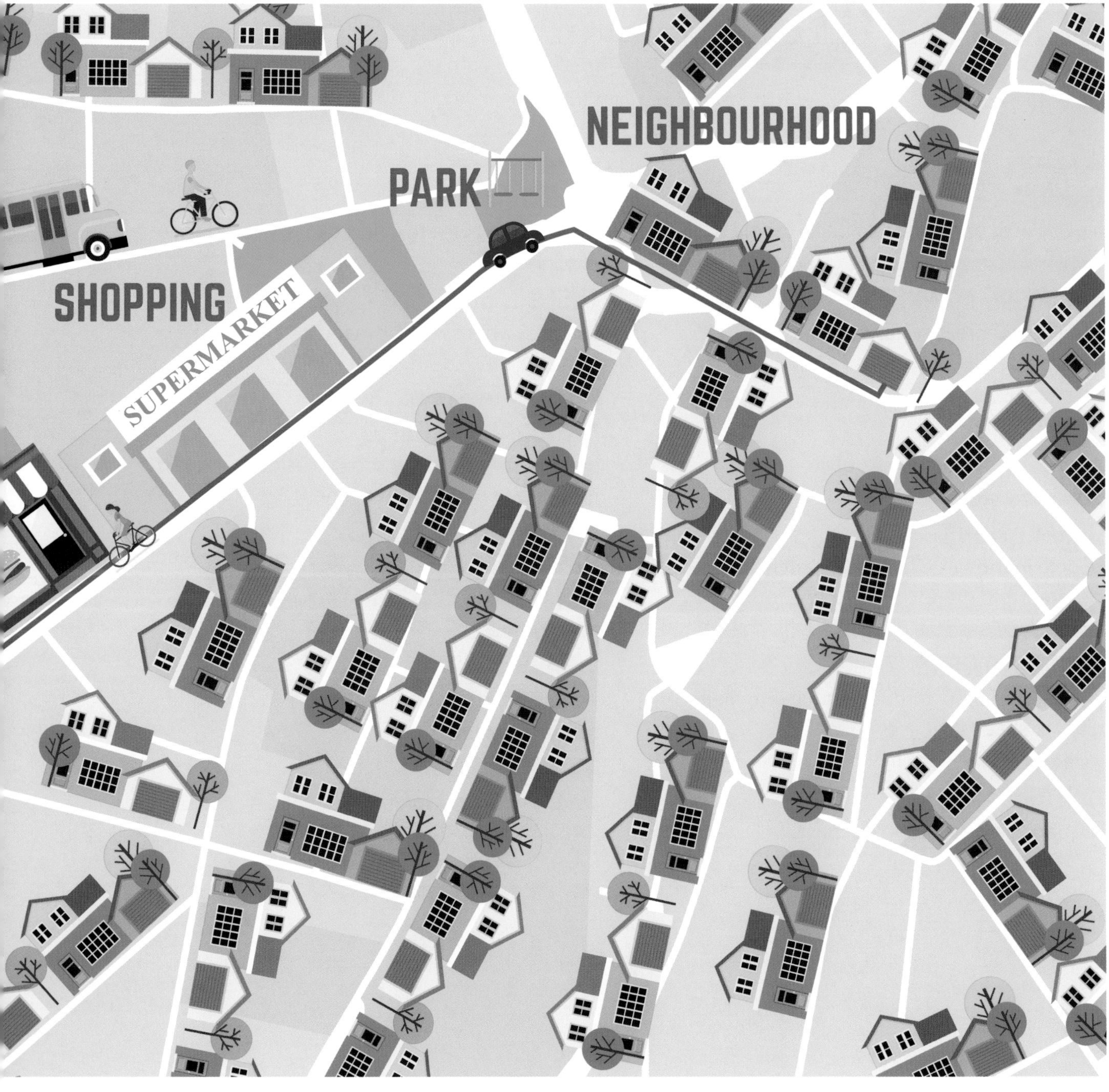

SHOPPING

SUPERMARKET

PARK

NEIGHBOURHOOD

GLOSSARY

CANOLA
a plant with seeds used to make canola oil

FARMERS' MARKET
a market where local farmers sell their fruit and vegetables

GALLERIES
businesses that sell works of art

GENERATIONS
people in the same family line, such as parents, children, and grandchildren

GLASSBLOWERS
people who blow through a tube into melted glass to shape it

HISTORICAL
relating to objects from the past

IMMIGRANTS
people who come to a new country to live there

MILLS
factories where wood is made into lumber or paper

NATIONAL PARKS
areas of special importance set aside and taken care of by a nation's government

RESIDENTS
people who live in a certain place

TOURISTS
people who travel for pleasure

VOLUNTEERS
people who work for free

TO LEARN MORE

BOOKS

Croza, Laurel. *I Know Here*. Toronto: Groundwood Books, 2013.

Falconer, Shelley and Shawna White. *Stones, Bones and Stitches: Storytelling through Inuit Art*. Toronto: Tundra Books, 2007.

Greenwood, Barbara and Jock MacRae. *The Kids Book of Canada*. Toronto: Kids Can Press, 2007.

Hacker, Carlotta. *The Kids Book of Canadian History*. Toronto: Kids Can Press, 2009.

Schwartz, Joanne. *Our Corner Grocery Store*. Toronto: Tundra Books, 2009.

WEBSITES

Canadian Geographic Kids Episodes: Explore Canada
www.canadiangeographic.ca/kids/cg_kids/default.asp

Kids' Stop: Indigenous and Northern Affairs Canada
www.aadnc-aandc.gc.ca/eng/1315444613519/1315444663239

National Geographic Kids: Canada
www.kids.nationalgeographic.com/explore/countries/canada

INDEX

ABOUT THE AUTHOR

Samantha Bell has written more than 40 nonfiction books for children. She enjoys small town living and would like to visit the many small towns of Canada.

JOBS IN SMALL TOWN CANADA

TRUE NORTH

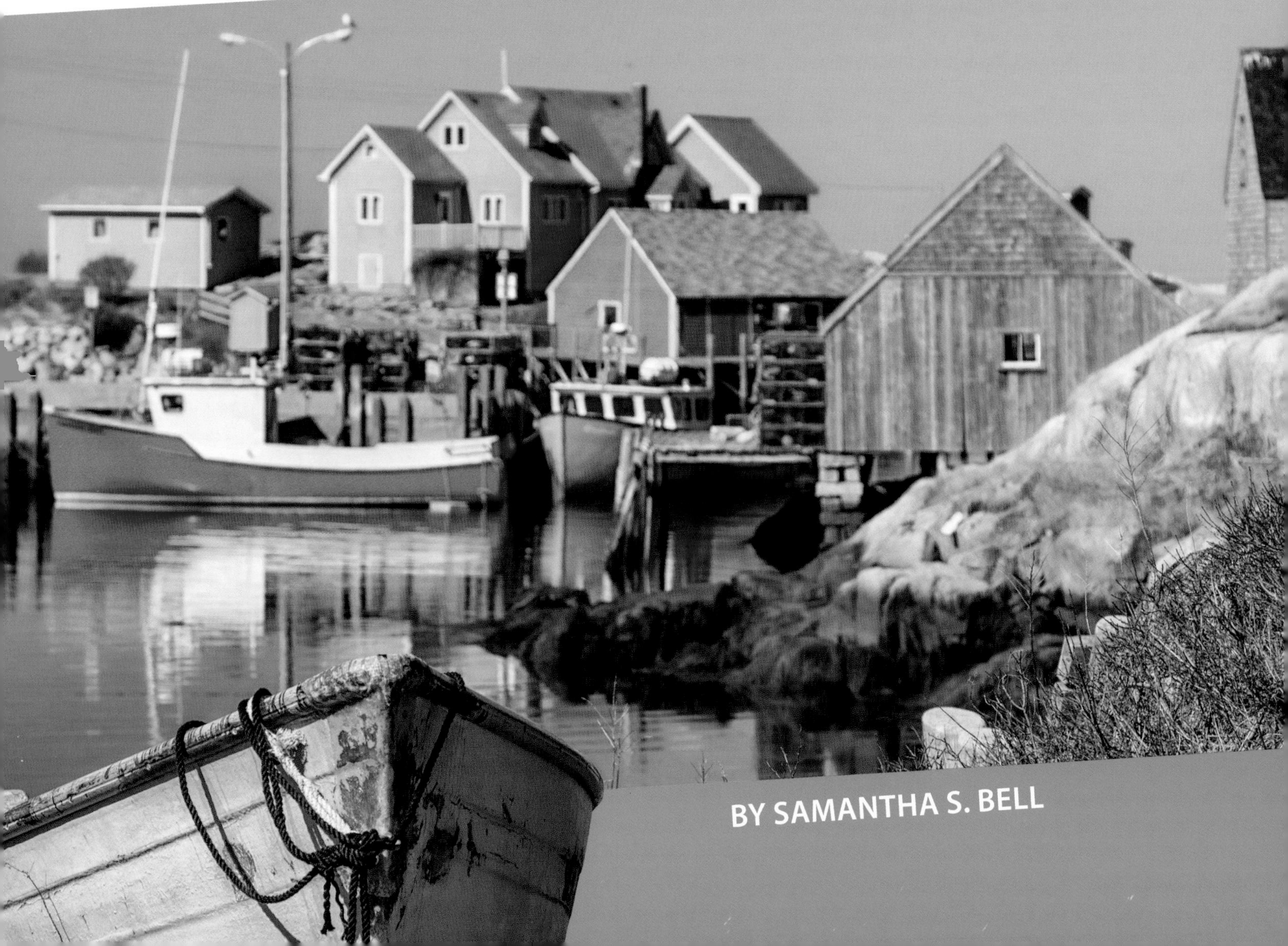

BY SAMANTHA S. BELL

True North is published by Beech Street Books
27 Stewart Rd. Collingwood, ON Canada L9Y 4M7

www.beechstreetbooks.ca

Produced by Red Line Editorial

Photographs ©: V. J. Matthew/Shutterstock Images, cover, 1; Elena Elisseeva/Shutterstock Images, 4–5; Paul McKinnon/Shutterstock Images, 6; Monkey Business Images/Shutterstock Images, 8–9; MarcPo/iStockphoto/Thinkstock, 10; Antonio Diaz/Shutterstock Images, 12–13; redfishweb/iStockphoto, 14–15; Les Palenik/Shutterstock Images, 16–17; Pierdelune/Shutterstock Images, 18; Red Line Editorial, 20–21

Editor: Heather C. Hudak
Designer: Laura Polzin

Library and Archives Canada Cataloguing in Publication

Bell, Samantha, author
       Jobs in small town Canada / by Samantha S. Bell.

(Working in Canadian communities)
Includes bibliographical references and index.
Issued in print and electronic formats.
ISBN 978-1-77308-026-0 (hardback).--ISBN 978-1-77308-054-3
(paperback).--ISBN 978-1-77308-082-6 (pdf).--ISBN 978-1-77308-110-6
(html)

       1. Occupations--Canada--Juvenile literature. 2. Small
cities--Canada--Juvenile literature. I. Title.

HF5382.5.C2B55 2016   j331.700971   C2016-903600-6
                                                  C2016-903601-4

Printed in the United States of America
Mankato, MN
August 2016

TABLE OF CONTENTS

Chapter One

SMALL TOWNS, BIG OPPORTUNITIES

Canada has cold, snowy mountains. It has many forests and wide-open prairies. It has rugged coastlines. In all of these places, people live and work together. Some of these people live in small towns.

A small town has fewer than 10,000 **residents**. That might sound like a lot. But the biggest city in Canada has more than six million residents.

People like living in small towns for many reasons. It is less expensive. Houses do not cost as much as in a big city. Food may be cheaper, too. A small town is not as noisy or as busy as a big city. There are no traffic jams. People usually do not stay out as late at night in

A fishing village in Newfoundland and Labrador

4